Common Core

Published by Gallopade International, Inc.
©Carole Marsh/Gallopade
Printed in the U.S.A. (Peachtree City, Georgia)

TABLE OF CONTENTS

G: Includes Graphic Organizer
GO: Graphic Organizer is also available 8½" x 11" online
download at www.gallopade.com/client/go
(numbers above correspond to the graphic organizer numbers online)

Why Do We Need Plants?

Read the text and answer the questions.

Think of the things we need to live. Nutritious food, clean air, and pure water make life possible for us. Other things—clothes, shelter, medicine, and energy—are also important. Do you realize that many things people need to survive come from plants?

Plants provide food. Only plants can convert the sun's light to food. Therefore, plants are known as <u>primary producers</u> and the foundation of most food webs on Earth. Many animals only eat plants. Humans eat plants, and even when we consume meat, we are eating food from animals that feed on plants like grass, corn, or oats.

Plants provide the air we breathe. When a plant converts sunlight to food, it takes in carbon dioxide and releases oxygen. Both humans and animals depend on that oxygen to survive. Plants also keep the gases balanced in the atmosphere so Earth has a livable climate.

Plants provide homes for animals. Many animals and insects live in or under trees and plants. They rely on plants for safety from predators. They also provide protection from wind and weather.

Plants preserve and form soil. Plant roots reduce <u>erosion</u> by holding topsoil together so more plants can grow. And when they die, plants help create soil. This occurs when the remains of plants mix with tiny particles of rock to form new soil. Plant remains give rich nutrients to the soil.

Plants provide useful products. People use plants for timber to build houses and for clothing to keep us warm and dry. About one quarter of our medicines come from plants. For example, aspirin is used to treat fevers and pain. It is derived from the bark of the willow tree. Fossil fuels—coal, oil, and natural gas—were formed by plants that decayed many millions of years ago. Today, we use those energy sources to make electricity, power our cars, and heat our homes.

Plants are beautiful. Plants provide joy and inspiration with their beauty. Imagine how bleak the world would be without trees, bushes, flowers, and other plants!

1. _____ Human beings existed long before plants.

2. _____ Plants are the basis of most of Earth's food webs.

3. _____ Trees are important for sheltering people and animals.

4. _____ Plants rely on humans to survive.

5. _____ Plants provide oxygen for people and animals to breathe.

PART B: Use the text to answer the questions.

6. A. Define <u>primary producer</u> as it is used in the text.
   B. Explain why plants are primary producers of food.

7. A. Use a dictionary to define <u>erosion</u> as it is used in the text.
   B. Explain how plants reduce erosion.

8. A. List 2 ways plants affect the air we breathe.
   B. Besides food, list 4 products that plants provide for people.

9. In Paragraph 2, find two words or phrases that are synonyms for *eat*.

PART C: Writing and research prompts

10. How many things in your home come from plants? List them and discuss your answers with the class.

11. Imagine you are an astronaut who has just arrived from a rocky, barren planet with no plants. Write a journal entry about your reaction to the beauty, color, and abundance of plants on Earth.

12. A. Divide the class into three groups: one to research each of the three main fossil fuels: coal, oil, and natural gas.
    B. Each group will use online and classroom resources to learn how the fossil fuel was formed, how it is used by people, and the consequences of its uses.
    C. Each group will create a computer presentation with illustrations, charts, etc., and share it with the class.
    D. As a class, discuss alternatives to using fossil fuels. Do any of them involve plants?

Structures of Plants

Read the text and answer the questions.

The two main classes of plants are nonvascular and vascular. Nonvascular plants are very simple plants, like mosses. Vascular plants are more complex. They have <u>specialized</u> tissues that perform <u>specific</u> functions, like carrying nutrients and water from one part of the plant to another.

Vascular plants have four basic structures: *roots*, *stems*, *leaves*, and *flowers*. Each structure has a special purpose.

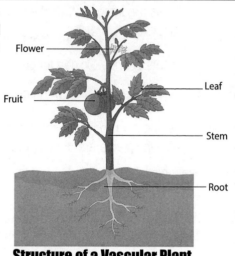

Structure of a Vascular Plant

Roots work themselves into the ground and draw water and minerals from soil. They also store extra food and keep the plant firmly anchored.

Stems can be bendable, like a lilac's stem, or stiff and woody, like a tree trunk. Not only does the stem support the plant, it also works as a plumbing system to move water and nutrients from the roots to the leaves and other plant structures.

Leaves are the food factories of the plant. They capture sunlight and carbon dioxide, which are combined with water inside the leaves to make glucose. Glucose is a sugar the plant uses for food. This process is called *photosynthesis*.

Flowers are the plant's reproductive organs. They contain tiny eggs, called ovules, and pollen. After the ovule is fertilized, it develops into a fruit to cover its seeds. Fruits can be hard, like a nut, or fleshy, like an apple.

1. What two structures in the illustration belong to the plant's reproductive system?

2. A. Which plant structure is below the ground? Explain its function.
   B. Does it need to be below ground to perform its functions? Why?

3. A. Which plant structures are above the ground? Explain their functions.
   B. Do they need to be above ground to perform their functions? Why?

4. List the four basic structures of a plant and explain how each is important to a plant's survival.

PART B: The foods below are specific parts of a plant: flower, fruit, leaf, stem, or root. Identify what part of a plant they represent.

5. Cabbage, lettuce, spinach _____

6. Carrot, potato, onion _____

7. Apple, tomato, pumpkin _____

8. Celery, asparagus _____

9. Corn, peas, lima beans _____

10. Cauliflower, broccoli _____

PART C: Use the text and other resources to answer the questions.

11. A. Use a dictionary to define specialized as it is used in the text.
    B. Use a dictionary to define specific as it is used in the text.
    C. Explain how the two words are similar and how they are different.

12. A. Find the simile in Paragraph 4. What two things are being compared?
    B. How does the simile helps you understand the stem's function?

13. A. Find the metaphor in Paragraph 5. What two things are being compared?
    B. How does the metaphor help you understand the function of leaves?

Plant Needs & Animal Needs

Use the graphic organizer to compare and contrast the basic needs of plants and the basic needs of animals.

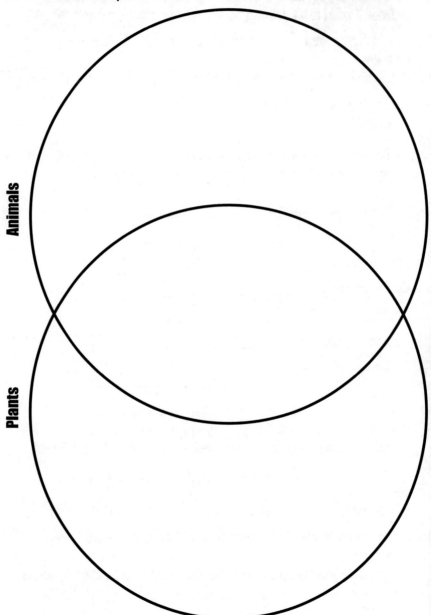

Animals

Plants

Plant Vocabulary

Fill in the chart with the definition for each word.

Vocabulary Word	Definition
flower	
fruit	
germinate	
leaf	
plant	
photosynthesis	
pollen	
root	
seed	
stem	

Garden to Cut Food Costs

During World War I and World War II, Americans were encouraged to garden and conserve food so the U.S. could ship food to American soldiers and needy Europeans.

Look at the poster and answer the questions.

1. What is the first thing you notice about the poster?

2. Who produced the poster? How do you know?

3. Who does Uncle Sam represent?

4. A. Who is the intended audience for this poster? How do you know?
   B. What is the poster trying to influence people to do? Why?
   C. What images help to communicate the poster's message?

5. Do you think this poster is effective in getting across its message? Why or why not?

6. Use classroom and online resources to find out whether Americans followed the poster's advice to create personal gardens and conserve food during World War I and World War II. Write a paragraph about what you learned.

Photosynthesis

Read the text and answer the questions.

Photosynthesis is a process that plants use to make their own food. Photosynthesis requires three things: carbon dioxide, water, and light. Plants collect carbon dioxide from the air and draw up water through their roots. The light they need comes from the sun!

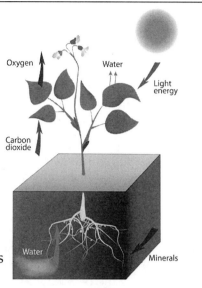

Photosynthesis takes place in <u>chloroplasts</u>, structures found in a plant's leaves. Inside the chloroplasts, a compound called <u>chlorophyll</u> absorbs sunlight.

Chloroplasts use the sunlight's energy to change carbon dioxide and water into simple sugars and oxygen. The plant's leaves release the oxygen and excess water into the air, and the plant uses the sugar as food. Extra food is stored throughout the plant, in its roots, stems, flowers, fruits, and leaves.

A simple way to demonstrate the process of photosynthesis is: Carbon Dioxide + Light + Water = Sugar + Oxygen.

1. A. Use online or classroom resources to look up the origins of the words <u>chloroplast</u> and <u>chlorophyll</u>.
   B. What does the root word "chloro" mean?

2. A. List 3 things a plant needs for photosynthesis to occur.
   B. What 2 things are created when photosynthesis occurs?

3. Write a letter to a friend explaining how plants make their own food.

4. Plants take in carbon dioxide and give off oxygen. What gases do humans and animals take in and exhale when they breathe? Research the answer. Explain how plants and humans/animals support each other.

Flowering Plant Life Cycle

Read the text and answer the questions.

Flowering plants are vascular plants that produce flowers to reproduce. Often, they produce seeds within a fruit. There is a specific life cycle for flowering plants.

Seeds are the beginning of life. Seeds have hard outer shells to protect the seed embryos inside. Once seeds fall to the ground, they need air, water, and soil to grow. *Germination* is the phase when seeds begin to grow. Usually, small roots are the first things to form.

A *sprout or seedling* is the first sign of life that appears above the soil, like a small stem with tiny leaves. A *mature plant* is a full-grown plant, with leaves, roots, and a stem.

Flowering happens when mature plants grow flowers, the plant's reproductive organs. Most flowers produce eggs in the pistil, the female organ, and produce pollen, the male substance that fertilizes the pistil. Pollination occurs when the wind, insects, or birds carry the powdery pollen from one plant and deposit it in another plant's flower, where it fertilizes the pistil. The flowers then produce seeds, and sometimes a fruit forms around the seeds.

Once the seeds fall to the ground, they anchor into the soil, and the cycle begins again.

1. Number (1-5) the phases of a flowering plant's life cycle.

__ flowering   __ seeds   __ mature plant   __ sprout   __ germination

2. Draw a diagram of the life cycle of a flowering plant. Label each stage of the plant's development.

3. Does a flowering plant's life cycle end once the seeds fall to the ground? Cite evidence from the text to support your answer.

4. Explain how insects, birds, and wind are important to the life cycle of a flowering plant.

5. As a class, plant some flower seeds. Keep a journal with photos to document the plant's cycle from seeds to flowering.

Invention of Velcro

Swiss engineer George de Mestral invented Velcro®. Read the fictional journal entry from 1948 and answer the questions.

> Today was a magnificent day spent hiking and hunting in the mountains with my dog. However, we were continually bothered by annoying cockleburs! At every turn, the pesky little burrs clung to my clothes and to my dog's fur.
>
> While struggling to pluck off the burrs, I became curious. How did they hang on so persistently? I took a closer look at them under my microscope. I was amazed at the sight! I saw hundreds of tiny hooks lining the surface, just waiting for someone to brush up against them. No wonder the burrs clung to everything in their path!
>
> And now, I have had an idea! Instead of fumbling with buttons or zippers on clothing, people could use fasteners made up of tiny hooks, just like those on the pesky burrs! It will take some time to develop my idea for manufacturing, but I already have a name for it. I shall call it "Velcro." The name is a combination of velvet and crochet, the French word for hook.
>
> I wonder if it shall be a success!

1. The ® symbol after Velcro stands for Registered Trademark. Research what that means and why it is important.

2. Summarize the main idea of the text.

3. Use online or classroom resources to find a photograph of a cocklebur plant. What part of the plant inspired the creation of Velcro—the leaf, stem, roots, or flower?

4. A. The invention of Velcro is an example of biomimicry. *Bio* means "life" and *mimic* means "imitation." Infer the definition of biomimicry and check a dictionary to see if you are correct.
B. Use online resources to find other examples of biomimicry that are used to make our lives easier.

Plant Products

People rely on plants for many important products. Divide into six groups, one for each category on the graphic organizer. Research products made from plants in each category. Present your lists to the class and discuss.

Food

_____

_____

_____

_____

_____

Shelter

_____

_____

_____

_____

_____

Plant

Medicine

_____

_____

_____

_____

_____

Clothing

_____

_____

_____

_____

_____

Products

Drinks

_____

_____

_____

_____

_____

Fuel

_____

_____

_____

_____

_____

The Food Web

Read the text, study the food web, and answer the questions.

Food webs show how plants and animals get their food, and the other animals that use them for food. A food web shows how plants and animals are interconnected and depend on one another for survival.

Primary producers in food webs are the plants that make their own food from sunlight. They are also called "autotrophs."

Primary consumers are the animals that eat primary producers. They are also known as "herbivores." Animals that eat primary consumers are known as *secondary consumers*.

FOOD WEB

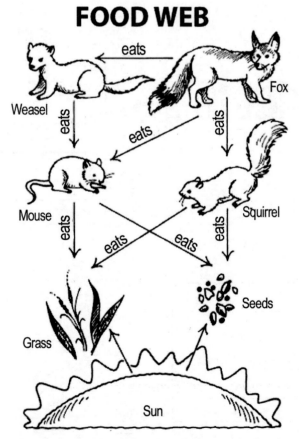

1. _____ Food webs show how plants and animals are connected.

2. _____ Food webs begin with sunlight.

3. _____ Plants are primary consumers.

4. _____ Grass and seeds grow with energy from the sun.

5. _____ Small animals eat larger animals in a food web.

PART B: Use the food webs to identify the primary producers, primary consumers, and secondary consumers

6. Grass _____

7. Mouse _____

8. Squirrel _____

9. Fox _____

10. Seeds _____

11. Weasel _____

PART C: Use the text to answer the questions.

12. What type of organisms are primary producers—plants or animals?

13. A. What is another name for a primary producer?
    B. Use a dictionary or online resource to find its Greek word origin.
    C. How does the word origin explain what a primary producer does?

14. A. What is another name for primary consumer?
    B. Use a dictionary or online resource to find its Latin word origin.
    C. How does the word origin explain what a primary consumer does?

PART D: Infer the answers from the text and illustrations.

15. Can a primary consumer sometimes be a secondary consumer? Explain your answer.

16. When are people primary consumers and when are they secondary consumers?

Plant Poetry

Read the poem and answer the questions.

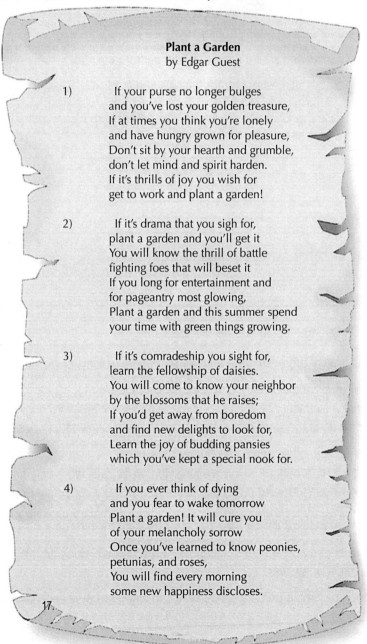

Plant a Garden
by Edgar Guest

1)   If your purse no longer bulges
and you've lost your golden treasure,
If at times you think you're lonely
and have hungry grown for pleasure,
Don't sit by your hearth and grumble,
don't let mind and spirit harden.
If it's thrills of joy you wish for
get to work and plant a garden!

2)   If it's drama that you sigh for,
plant a garden and you'll get it
You will know the thrill of battle
fighting foes that will beset it
If you long for entertainment and
for pageantry most glowing,
Plant a garden and this summer spend
your time with green things growing.

3)   If it's comradeship you sight for,
learn the fellowship of daisies.
You will come to know your neighbor
by the blossoms that he raises;
If you'd get away from boredom
and find new delights to look for,
Learn the joy of budding pansies
which you've kept a special nook for.

4)   If you ever think of dying
and you fear to wake tomorrow
Plant a garden! It will cure you
of your melancholy sorrow
Once you've learned to know peonies,
petunias, and roses,
You will find every morning
some new happiness discloses.

17.

1. What is the tone of the poem? Does it inspire hope or sorrow?

2. A. What is the message of the poem?
   B. Who is the intended audience of the poem?
   C. Do you think the poet presents his message well? Why or why not?

3. A. What is the poet's opinion of gardening?
   B. Do you agree with the poet? What is your opinion of gardening?

PART B: Answer the questions and write the number(s) of the stanza(s) that offer the answer(s).

4. _____ What kind of thrill does a garden offer?

5. _____ How can you learn about your neighbor?

6. _____ What can a garden cure?

PART C: Use your own words to explain what the poet meant by the following phrases.

7. "your purse no longer bulges" _____

8. "foes that will beset it" _____

9. "pageantry most glowing" _____

10. "the fellowship of daisies" _____

PART D: Writing prompts

11. A. Does the poem make you want to start growing your own garden? Why or why not?
    B. Imagine you have a large backyard, perfect for a garden. Describe and draw the garden you would like to grow. Include plants (like vegetables or flowers) as well as statues, fountains, or other features.

12. A. As a class, use online resources to find "Gardening," another poem by Edgar Guest. Read the poem aloud in class. Discuss the different points of view of the two poems.
    B. Write an acrostic poem using the word "gardening." Illustrate your poem and display it on posterboard.

Passing On Traits

Read the text and answer the questions.

It is easy to see that children have many of the same traits as their parents. Did you know the same is true of plants?

Before the 1800s, no one understood how parents passed traits to their children. In the 1860s, an Austrian monk named Gregor Mendel made an important discovery.

While raising pea plants, Mendel observed that some pea plants were *tall* and others were *short*. He saw that some pea plants produced *yellow* peas while others produced *green* peas. And some pea plants produced *smooth* peas while others produced *wrinkled* peas. He wondered, "What causes these differences?"

To investigate the cause of these differences, Mendel planned an experiment. He took a *tall* pea plant and cross-pollinated it with a *short* pea plant to see what kind of offspring they produced.

One *tall* parent and one *short* parent produced four *tall* offspring. "Strange," Mendel thought, "why did the trait for *tall* appear and the trait for *short* disappear?" He tried crossing a plant with *smooth* peas and a plant with *wrinkled* peas, and produced offspring with only *smooth* peas. When he crossed *green* pea plants with *yellow* pea plants, only *green* pea plants were produced.

Mendel concluded that each trait is controlled by two "invisible factors," called "alleles." An offspring gets one allele from each parent. He also determined that one allele can mask, or cover up, the other. He called the allele that appeared "dominant" and the allele that disappeared "recessive."

---

1. A. What observations did Mendel make about pea plants?
   B. What question did Mendel ask based upon his observations?
   C. Describe Mendel's experiment with peas.
   D. What was the purpose of Mendel's experiment with peas?
   E. Describe the results of Mendel's experiments.

2. What conclusions did Mendel draw from his results?

3. A. What is the difference between "dominant" and "recessive"?
   B. List the recessive and dominant alleles for each experiment.

Christmas in Korea

A Christmas tree has special meaning for many Americans. It can be an important symbol to soldiers many miles away from home during Christmastime.

Look at the photo and answer the questions.

U.S. Soldiers in Korea—December 1951   Courtesy of U.S. Army

1. What do you notice first when you look at the photograph?

2. Why are the soldiers setting up a ladder?

3. What does the photograph reveal about the physical surroundings? Does it look cold or warm? It is a welcoming place or a dismal one?

4. What does the tree symbolize to soldiers who are away from home at Christmastime?

5. Imagine you are a soldier in the photo, far away from home during the holidays. Write a letter to your family. Tell them about the tree you and your buddies found and decorated. Proofread and edit your work.

CAUSE AND EFFECT

Plant Adaptations

Read the text, answer the questions and fill in the graphic organizer.

Over a long period of time, plants develop special features that allow them to survive in many different habitats. One example is how the golden barrel cactus has adapted to life in the desert.

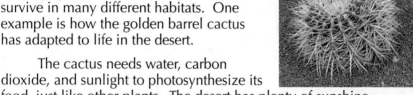

The cactus needs water, carbon dioxide, and sunlight to photosynthesize its food, just like other plants. The desert has plenty of sunshine, but little water. The spines of the cactus are a special type of leaf that collects and conserves water. The spines are very prickly and protect the cactus from animals that try to eat it.

The cactus has developed the ability to <u>swell</u> and store water when it rains. When it gets very dry, the cactus can contract and become dormant, or inactive. It then springs back to life once the rain returns. The cactus has also adapted so it can live on the limited nutrients in the sandy soil of the desert.

1. Use a dictionary to define <u>swell</u> as it is used in the text. List a synonym and an antonym.

2. Complete the Cause/Effect diagram for the golden barrel cactus.

Effect:

Cause:
Dry desert climate

Effect:

Effect:

3. Use online and classroom resources to research plants that have adapted to other harsh environments. Create a computer presentation with photographs to present to the class.

Crop Rotation Solution

Read the text and answer the questions.

After the Civil War, farmers in the southern United States had problems growing healthy crops. Many years of growing cotton and tobacco had <u>depleted</u> the soil and left it with few nutrients.

George Washington Carver was an American scientist who had a solution—crop rotation. He convinced southern farmers to plant peanuts in their fields. Peanuts <u>enriched</u> the soil by replenishing the nitrogen that had been stripped from it.

Crop rotation worked well. Farmers planted peanuts in a field one year, and then planted cotton in the same field the following year. By continuing the rotation of peanuts and cotton crops, the soil stayed fertile and produced bountiful harvests. Carver also found other crops to rotate such as peas and sweet potatoes.

After awhile, the farmers had a new problem. They were not being paid much for their peanuts. In fact, there were so many peanuts that many of them were rotting in warehouses. What could they do with all those peanuts?

George Washington Carver tackled that problem next.

1. A. Use a dictionary to define <u>deplete</u> as it is used in the text.
   B. Use a dictionary to define <u>enrich</u> as it is used in the text.
   C. Are the words synonyms or antonyms?

2. Infer why so many farmers grew cotton and tobacco in the South.

3. List the benefits of crop rotation.

4. Create a graphic organizer to answer the following questions.
   A. What was the problem Carver was trying to solve?
   B. Whose problem was it?
   C. Describe Carver's solution and its results.

5. Use online and classroom resources to research George Washington Carver's solutions for the abundance of peanuts. Work in small groups. Describe his solutions and display photographs or illustrations of them.

Endangering Plants

Individually or in small groups, complete the graphic organizer to propose a solution for one or more of the following problems threatening plants.

Pollution   **Invasive Species**   **Deforestation**

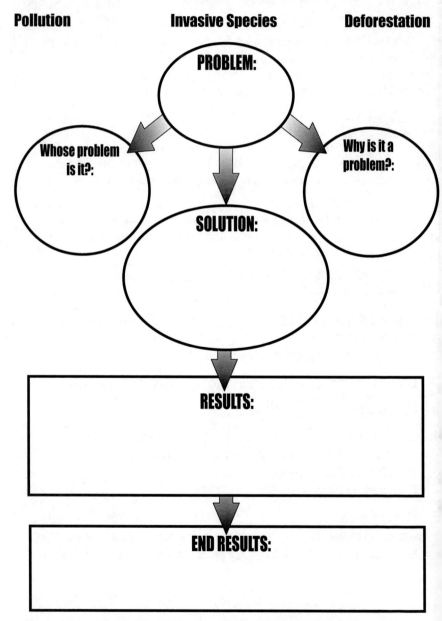

PROBLEM:

Whose problem is it?:

Why is it a problem?:

SOLUTION:

RESULTS:

END RESULTS:

Environmental Factors

Read the text and answer the questions.

There are four basic factors in a plant's environment that will affect how it grows: light, temperature, water, and nutrition.

Light—The amount and intensity of light that a plant receives is important. If it does not get enough light, it may not be able to photosynthesize enough food. Light that is too harsh can damage it.

Temperature—Hardy plants can withstand cooler temperatures, but plants cannot absorb water if the ground is frozen. Low temperatures can slow a plant's growth or cause it to go dormant. Plants need a safe range of temperatures to flower or develop fruit.

Water—Plants need water, both in the soil for its roots to absorb, and in the humidity of the air around the plant. Too little water will cause a plant to wither, and too much will drown the plant.

Nutrients—Just like people, plants need good nutrition. There are 18 different elements that a plant needs, including carbon, nitrogen, and hydrogen. If a plant does not get all the nutrients it needs, it will not grow strong or stay healthy.

1. A. Use online and classroom resources to define humidity.
   B. Find a synonym for humidity.

2. What are the four basic environmental factors that affect a plant's growth?

3. Circle other factors that could affect a plant's growth.
   a. bugs   b. pesticides   c. polluted water

4. Predict what would happen if a rose bush grew in too cool an environment.

5. Predict what would happen if a field of corn got too little water.

6. A. Choose one of the four factors that affect a plant's growth. Design an experiment that shows how that factor affects a plant.
   B. Write out the experiment, step by step. Predict the results.
   C. Conduct the experiment. Keep a daily journal of your observations.
   D. Did the results match your predictions? Explain.

Correlations to Common Core State Standards

For your convenience, correlations are listed page-by-page and for the entire book!

This book is correlated to the <u>Common Core State Standards for English Language Arts</u> grades 3-8, and to <u>Common Core State Standards for Literacy in History, Science, & Technological Subjects</u> grades 6-8.

Correlations are highlighted in gray.

PAGE #	READING — Includes: RI: Reading Informational Text / RH: Reading History	WRITING — Includes: W: Writing / WHST: Writing History, Science, & Technology	LANGUAGE — Includes: L: Language / LF: Language Foundational Skills	SPEAKING & LISTENING — Includes: SL: Speaking & Listening
2-3	RI/RH . 1 2 3 4 5 6 7 8 9 10	W/WHST . 1 2 3 4 5 6 7 8 9 10	L/LF . 1 2 3 4 5 6	SL . 1 2 3 4 5 6
4-5	RI/RH . 1 2 3 4 5 6 7 8 9 10	W/WHST . 1 2 3 4 5 6 7 8 9 10	L/LF . 1 2 3 4 5 6	SL . 1 2 3 4 5 6
6	RI/RH . 1 2 3 4 5 6 7 8 9 10	W/WHST . 1 2 3 4 5 6 7 8 9 10	L/LF . 1 2 3 4 5 6	SL . 1 2 3 4 5 6
7	RI/RH . 1 2 3 4 5 6 7 8 9 10	W/WHST . 1 2 3 4 5 6 7 8 9 10	L/LF . 1 2 3 4 5 6	SL . 1 2 3 4 5 6
8	RI/RH . 1 2 3 4 5 6 7 8 9 10	W/WHST . 1 2 3 4 5 6 7 8 9 10	L/LF . 1 2 3 4 5 6	SL . 1 2 3 4 5 6
9	RI/RH . 1 2 3 4 5 6 7 8 9 10	W/WHST . 1 2 3 4 5 6 7 8 9 10	L/LF . 1 2 3 4 5 6	SL . 1 2 3 4 5 6
10	RI/RH . 1 2 3 4 5 6 7 8 9 10	W/WHST . 1 2 3 4 5 6 7 8 9 10	L/LF . 1 2 3 4 5 6	SL . 1 2 3 4 5 6
11	RI/RH . 1 2 3 4 5 6 7 8 9 10	W/WHST . 1 2 3 4 5 6 7 8 9 10	L/LF . 1 2 3 4 5 6	SL . 1 2 3 4 5 6
12-13	RI/RH . 1 2 3 4 5 6 7 8 9 10	W/WHST . 1 2 3 4 5 6 7 8 9 10	L/LF . 1 2 3 4 5 6	SL . 1 2 3 4 5 6
14-15	RI/RH . 1 2 3 4 5 6 7 8 9 10	W/WHST . 1 2 3 4 5 6 7 8 9 10	L/LF . 1 2 3 4 5 6	SL . 1 2 3 4 5 6
16-17	RI/RH . 1 2 3 4 5 6 7 8 9 10	W/WHST . 1 2 3 4 5 6 7 8 9 10	L/LF . 1 2 3 4 5 6	SL . 1 2 3 4 5 6
18	RI/RH . 1 2 3 4 5 6 7 8 9 10	W/WHST . 1 2 3 4 5 6 7 8 9 10	L/LF . 1 2 3 4 5 6	SL . 1 2 3 4 5 6
19	RI/RH . 1 2 3 4 5 6 7 8 9 10	W/WHST . 1 2 3 4 5 6 7 8 9 10	L/LF . 1 2 3 4 5 6	SL . 1 2 3 4 5 6
20	RI/RH . 1 2 3 4 5 6 7 8 9 10	W/WHST . 1 2 3 4 5 6 7 8 9 10	L/LF . 1 2 3 4 5 6	SL . 1 2 3 4 5 6
21	RI/RH . 1 2 3 4 5 6 7 8 9 10	W/WHST . 1 2 3 4 5 6 7 8 9 10	L/LF . 1 2 3 4 5 6	SL . 1 2 3 4 5 6
22	RI/RH . 1 2 3 4 5 6 7 8 9 10	W/WHST . 1 2 3 4 5 6 7 8 9 10	L/LF . 1 2 3 4 5 6	SL . 1 2 3 4 5 6
23	RI/RH . 1 2 3 4 5 6 7 8 9 10	W/WHST . 1 2 3 4 5 6 7 8 9 10	L/LF . 1 2 3 4 5 6	SL . 1 2 3 4 5 6
COMPLETE BOOK	RI/RH . 1 2 3 4 5 6 7 8 9 10	W/WHST . 1 2 3 4 5 6 7 8 9 10	L/LF . 1 2 3 4 5 6	SL . 1 2 3 4 5 6

For the complete Common Core standard identifier, combine your grade + "." + letter code above + "." + number code above.

In addition to the correlations indicated here, the activities may be adapted or expanded to align to additional standards and to meet the diverse needs of your unique students!